Turkey Talk

What's That Smell?!

Honey Jacobs

Shhh...

ON
AIR

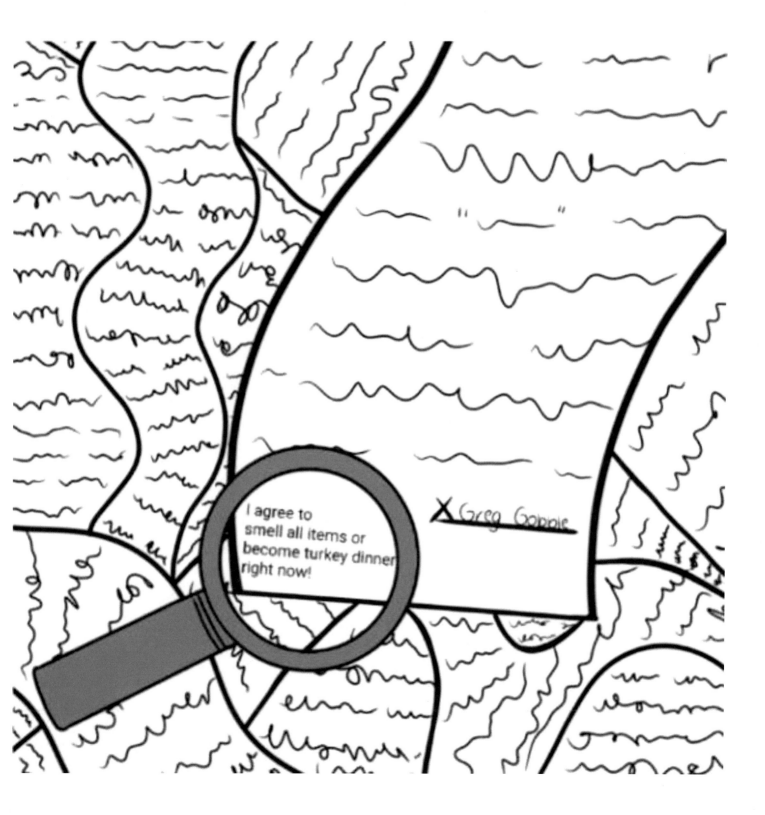

Oh butterball, that sounds like my famous firecracker casserole.

Famous fire-whata?

Famous firecracker casserole. Everytime someone tries it, they explode like a firecracker from excitement!

Yeah! Sure. Excitement ...

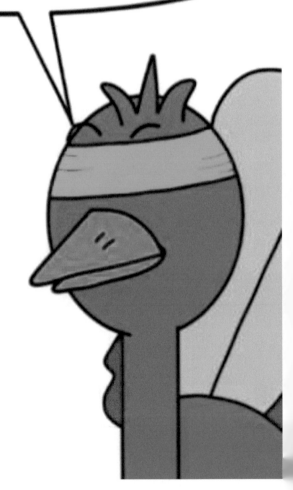

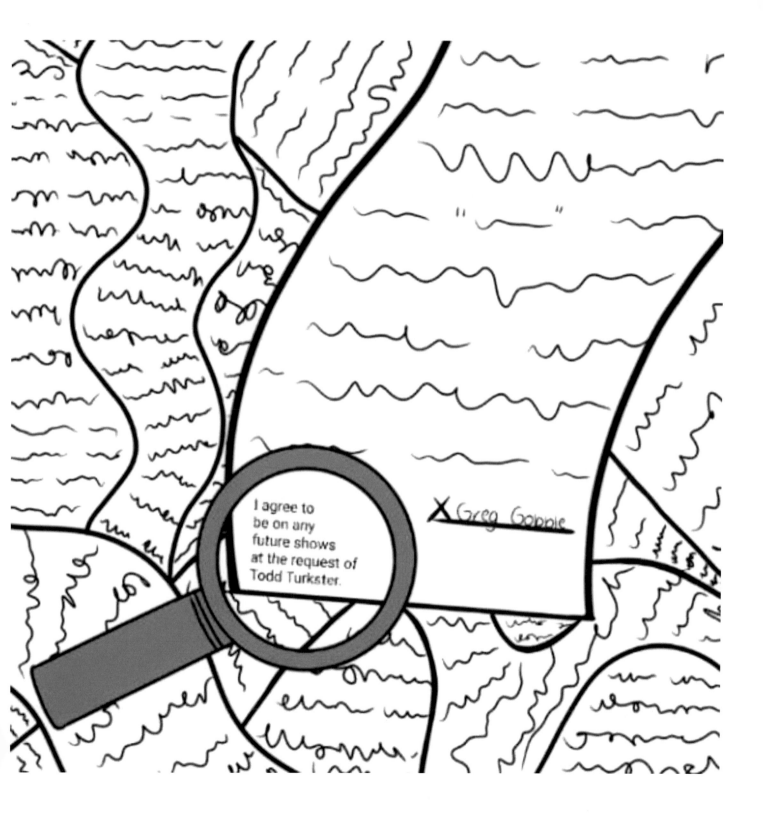

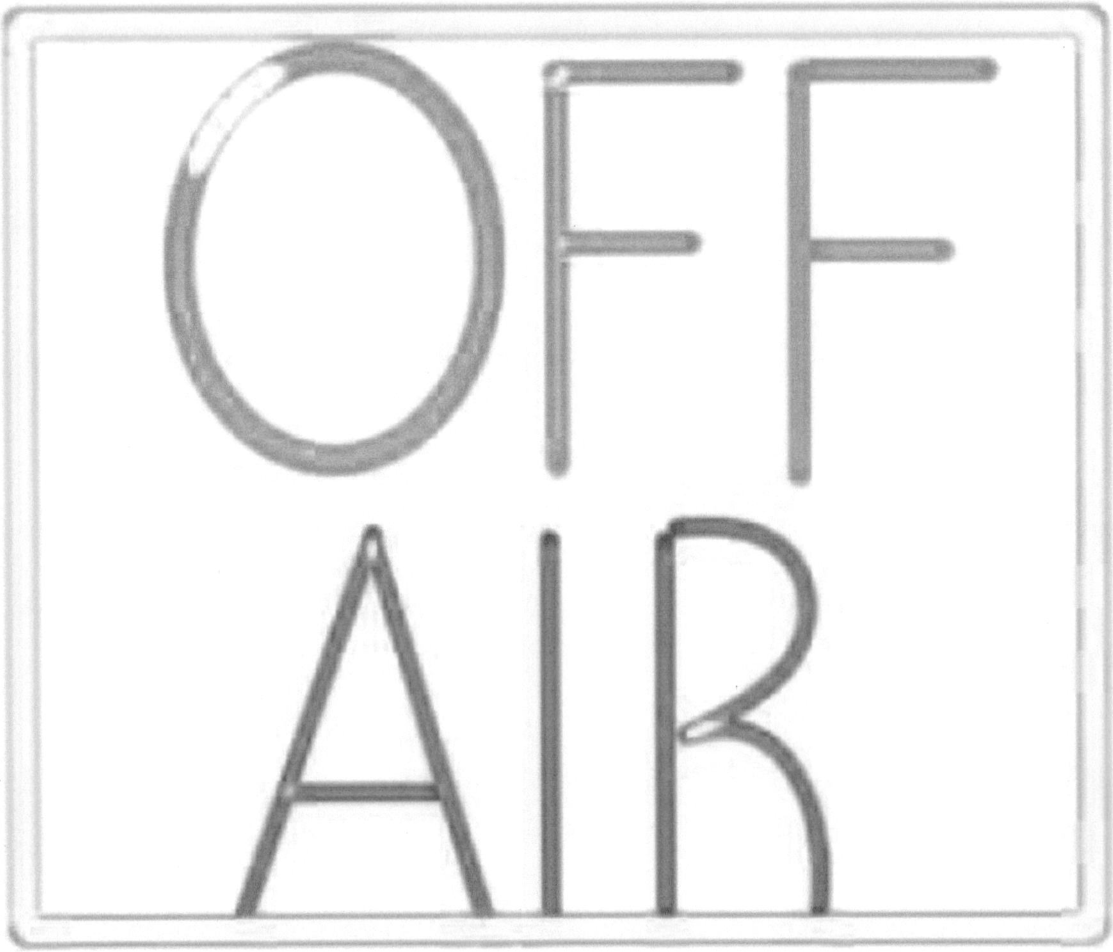
OFF
AIR